How to Make a Quilt – Log Cabin Quilt Pattern

By Rose Smith

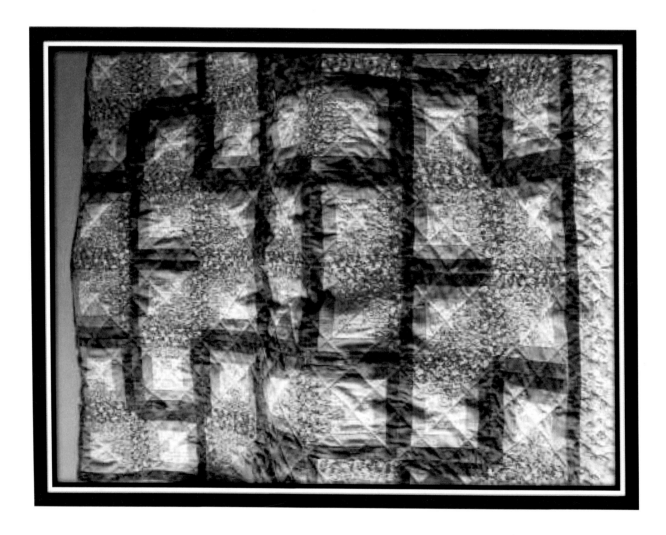

Table of Contents

Introduction

Quilting is a wonderfully satisfying hobby. It has grown in popularity over the last few decades but many people still feel that it looks too complicated for them. They lack the confidence to take the first steps towards making a patchwork quilt.

What I am hoping to show you through this book is that quilting is not a difficult craft as long as you break the project down into small steps. By following the step by step instructions you can make an easy log cabin quilt that will wow your friends. The finished size of this quilt is 72.1/2" by 83".

The log cabin quilt block is one of the oldest quilt blocks known. Traditionally, it was made with a red or yellow square in the middle to signify the hearth of the log cabin. The 'logs' of the cabin are then added around the central square using strips of fabric. These strips can be added in a clockwise or anti clockwise direction – the important thing is to stick to one way within each block. Usually there are two light logs and two dark logs in each round of logs. That makes it possible to make wonderful designs by forming patterns using the contrast between the light and dark.

For this quilt I have used the same colour fabrics throughout but I have chosen two different versions of the log cabin block. One is a straightforward traditional log cabin and the other is a variation known as the courthouse steps quilt block. They are both very simple to make but just give a little more variation to the quilt. I always think that it is important for a quilt to give plenty for the eye to look at.

Seams in this quilt are always ¼". Accuracy is important so one easy way is to mark your sewing machine ¼" away from the needle so that you know to line up the edges of the fabric with that mark.

Seam allowances are usually pressed towards one side – the darker fabric if possible. However in a log cabin quilt the seam allowances should always be pressed away from the middle. You can see how neat it makes the back of the quilt which will help make the quilt top nice and flat when it is finished.

In addition, it will help the blocks a lot if you press after each log has been added. Try and place your ironing board somewhere near where you are working to save yourself a lot of time.

Accuracy in cutting is just as important as accuracy in sewing, so do take care when cutting your strips of fabric. A rotary cutter, mat and ruler do help a lot with this.

The most important thing to remember is to enjoy yourself. This quilt will be your project, so don't beat yourself up if you make a mistake – at worst you might need to unpick a few seams and at best you can say that the mistake is a design feature! I find quilting enormously satisfying and I hope that you will agree with me when you have made this quilt.

Fabric Requirements

This log cabin block is based on 2" wide strips of fabric of varying length. I have listed the total fabric requirement in each fabric rounded up to the nearest ¼ yard. Some people may prefer to cut a number of 2" strips and then just cut the lengths they need as they go along. Others may prefer to cut all the strips before beginning sewing, so I have listed all the strips required here:

Cream and light blue fabrics:

Two strips 2" wide by the full width of fabric in both cream and light blue. These are sewn together before cutting. You will need a further twenty strips of light blue 3.1/2" long in the quilt and seven 2" strips in both the cream and the light blue for the borders.

Total requirement in cream: nine 2" strips (**1/2 yard**).

Total requirement in light blue: eleven 2" strips (**3/4 yard**).

Light brown (yellow) fabric:

3.1/2" strips: sixty

5" strips: forty

Additional seven 2" strips for the border

Total requirement in yellow: seventeen 2" strips (**1 yard**)

Medium blue fabric:

5" strips: forty

6.1/2" strips: twenty

Total requirement in medium blue: nine 2" strips (**1/2 yard**)

Medium brown fabric:

6.1/2" strips: sixty

8" strips: forty

Total requirement in medium brown: eighteen 2" strips (**1 yard**)

Dark blue fabric:

8" strips: forty

9.1/2" strips: twenty

Total requirement in dark blue: thirteen 2" strips (**3/4 yard**)

Dark brown fabric:

9.1/2" strips: sixty strips

11" strips: forty strips

Two 11" squares

Total requirement in dark brown: twenty nine 2" strips and two 11" squares (**2 yards**)

Binding, backing and wadding

For the binding you will need a further eight 2.1/2" strips of a new fabric. My binding is black (**3/4 yard**).

For the backing you will need two rectangles of fabric 76" long cut across the width of fabric (**2.1/4 yards of each**).

For the wadding you will need a rectangle 76" by 88" approximately.

Fabric Selection

One of the delights of log cabin quilts is the designs that can be formed from varying the colours, allowing them to fade from dark to light within each block.

For the blocks in this log cabin quilt I have chosen a very light blue fabric for the middle of each block. It is light enough to be just off white and I am going to refer to it as cream throughout the pattern to avoid confusion with the three blues used in the block. For the surrounding logs I have chosen three shades of blue - dark, medium and light – and three brown fabrics – again dark, medium and light although In fact for the light brown I have used yellow.

Making the traditional log cabin blocks

This is the traditional log cabin quilt block and it measures 11" square at this stage. When you allow for the fact that ¼" on each side will be used up in seam allowance when the quilt blocks are sewn together, you'll see that this square will be 10.1/2" wide in the quilt. It is known as a 10.1/2" block even though it is 11" when you complete it.

Both the central square and all the strips of fabric around it are cut at 2" wide. Because of the seam allowances as mentioned above, these strips of fabric will be 1.1/2" wide when sewn in place. So the first thing to do is cut strips of fabric 2" wide across the width of fabric. This means that they will be approximately 42" long and you can then cut the lengths that you need from these long strips of fabric.

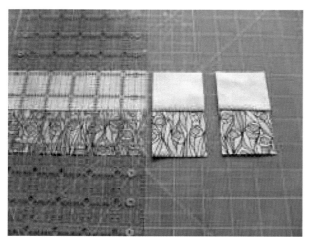

Sew together one strip of the cream central fabric and one strip of the light blue fabric that forms the first log. Press the seam allowance away from the cream central square (towards the darker of the two fabrics in this case) and cut at 2" intervals. This will give you a small strip which is made up of a square each of the two fabrics. These will form the central square of the log cabin block and the first log. You will need forty of these altogether.

Cut a 3.1/2" length of the light blue fabric and place it to the right of the pair of squares. Sew it to the two squares. You have now added the second log. Each round of logs will consist of two blue and two brown strips of fabric.

The next two logs will be light brown. You will need one which is 3.1/2" long to sew across the top and one which is 5" long to sew down the left hand side. That is one complete round of logs completed – the next round will be made using the medium blue and medium brown fabrics.

Cut two lengths of medium blue fabric, one 5" long to sew across the bottom and one 6.1/2" long to sew to the right hand side of the block.

Cut two lengths of medium brown fabric, one 6.1/2" long to sew across the top and one 8" long to sew to the left hand side of the block. That will complete the second round of logs. The next round will be made using the dark blue and dark brown fabrics and that will complete this version of the log cabin quilt block.

From the dark blue fabric cut two lengths, one 8" long to sew to the bottom of the block and one 9.1/2" long to sew to the right hand side.

From the dark brown fabric cut two lengths, one 9.1/2" long to sew to the top of the block and one 11" long to sew to the left hand side of the block.

That completes the first version of the log cabin quilt block. You need to make nineteen more of these to give you twenty blocks in total.

Making the Courthouse Steps Quilt Block

The courthouse steps quilt block is made in exactly the same way as the traditional log cabin, but there are three brown and one blue log in each round. The previous block had two logs each of blue and brown in each round of logs.

Once again begin with a strip each of cream and light blue sewn together and cut at 2" intervals to give you the central square and the first log. The second log is made using a yellow strip 3.1/2" long sewn to the right hand side of the block.

The next two logs are still yellow – one 3.1/2" long sewn across the top of the block and one 5" long sewn to the left hand side of the block.

The second round of logs is made with a 5" medium blue strip across the bottom of the block and then three medium brown logs: one 6.1/2" long for the right hand side of the block, one 6.1/2" long for the top and one 8" long for the left hand side of the block.

Finally the third round of logs is made with one 8" strip of dark blue fabric across the bottom of the block followed by three dark brown logs: one 9.1/2" long for the right hand side of the block, one 9.1/2" long for the top and one 11" long for the left hand side.

That completes the courthouse steps quilt block and you will again need to make nineteen more of them to give twenty blocks in total.

Assembling the log cabin quilt top

The quilt blocks are sewn together in seven rows of six blocks each. In addition to the forty log cabin and courthouse steps blocks you will need two 11" dark brown squares. The blocks are all mixed up to make the pattern and they are also rotated in different directions, so I am going to show you each row individually to make it more clear.

The first row (at the top of the photo) is made with a log cabin block at each end and two in the middle with a courthouse steps on either side of the middle pair. Note where the quilt blocks have been rotated to give particular blocks of colour.

The second row is made with two log cabin blocks in the middle and two courthouse steps on either side – you will need to check with the photo to be sure that you have the blocks facing in the correct directions.

The third row is made with a log cabin block at each end and two of them in the middle. There is again a courthouse steps block on either side of the middle pair of blocks.

Row four has the two dark brown squares at each end with three courthouse steps blocks in between them.

Row five is the same as row one with four log cabin blocks and two courthouse steps blocks.

Row six is the same as row two with two log cabin blocks in the middle and two courthouse steps block on each side.

Finally row seven is the same as row three, but this time the two courthouse steps blocks are pointing in towards the middle.

Sew the blocks together across each row and then sew the rows together. At this stage your quilt should measure 63.1/2" wide by 74" long.

Making the log cabin quilt border

For the quilt border I have used some of the fabrics from within the quilt. All of the blocks around the edge of the quilt have a dark brown strip of fabric on the edge so that is almost like having the first border made of dark brown.

The first true border is made using 2" strips of the light blue fabric. You will need two strips 63.1/2" long to sew to the top and bottom of the quilt and two lengths of 77" for the sides.

It is very tempting to join two strips of light blue fabric together, sew them to the top of the quilt and then cut across the strip at the corner of the quilt. I will admit (in a whisper), that I have done this in the past. This saves time but it does not give the same finish as putting the border on in the correct way and you may end up with a wavy border.

The correct method of adding a quilt border is to measure the width of the quilt at the top, the middle and the bottom. As long as those measurements are not too different from each other, you can take the average of those three measurements for the width of your quilt and cut two border strips to that length. Pin each end of the border to the quilt edge, then pin the midpoint and then find the midpoint between the ends and the middle. In this way you will be able to ease the border and the quilt edge as you sew them together so that both the top and the bottom will be the same length.

If your three measurements had not been anything like each other, you would need to look at options such as trimming the quilt top where necessary.

Repeat the three measurements to find the length of the quilt and make two lengths of the light blue fabric to sew to the sides of the quilt.

The second quilt border is made using 2" strips of yellow fabric – you'll remember that this is the light brown fabric. Make two lengths of 66.1/2" (or whatever the measurements for your quilt are) to sew to the top and bottom of the quilt and two lengths of 80" for the sides.

Finally the third border is made using the very light fabric that I have called cream, used for the central square in all the log cabin quilt blocks. You will need two lengths of 69.1/2" for the top and bottom of the quilt and two lengths of 83" for the sides of the quilt.

That completes the top of the log cabin quilt. It could do with a good press to tidy up all the seam allowances which may have flapped the wrong way during all the handling that the quilt has had.

Log Cabin Quilt Backing

The quilt is now ready to be layered with the backing fabric and wadding. These need to be larger than the quilt top. I normally allow 2" extra all the way round so that the backing fabric will measure 4" greater in both width and length. This is for two reasons: one because the process of quilting can slightly change the quilt top measurements and the second reason is that I find it easier to layer the quilt when there is a bit of spare backing fabric. No matter how careful you are you may well find that the quilt top doesn't lie completely straight on the backing. For these reasons, the backing and the wadding need to be rectangles about 80" by 90". I've rounded these measurements up slightly just to give easier numbers to work with.

Both of the measurements of the quilt top are greater than one width of fabric, so you will need to sew together fabric pieces for the backing. I have chosen to use two strips of fabric in different colours but from the same range.

Cut one 76" length of both fabrics and sew them together along the 76" length. This will give you one piece of fabric 76" by about 88" (that's the two widths of fabric sewn together side by side).

Press carefully – time taken now will save you time and heartache later by giving you a flat backing to work with. I pressed the seams open on my backing to make it extra flat. Not everyone likes using starch, but I find that it really does help to give a bit of body to your backing so that it is more likely to stay in place and not rumple when you are quilting. Spray starch on one side of the backing and then iron on the other side so that you don't get starch all over your iron.

Layering the Quilt

Lay the backing on the work surface with right side down and smooth gently from the middle outwards. Lay the wadding on top and again smooth gently. Finally lay the patchwork quilt top with right side up.

Many quilters recommend fastening the edges of the quilt backing in some way to keep it taut before you add the next two layers, but I have to say that I find this very difficult and it just doesn't work for me. You could tape the edges of the backing to the work surface (floor in my case), using masking tape. If you have a table large enough for you to be layering the quilt on it, you might be able to use clips to hold the edges of the quilt in place. I offer these as options, but find that I can achieve the results I need by being carefully with smoothing each layer as I put it down. When I have finished smoothing the three layers, I always flip the quilt so that the backing is on top and give that one extra smoothing before turning it right side up and basting it.

Begin in the middle of the quilt and smooth gently away from the middle up and down and to the sides using gentle sweeping motions of your hands. To baste the three layers together I usually use quilting pins.

These are safety pins with a slightly curved arm so that they can cope with the thickness of three layers of fabric. Place pins at about four inch intervals, again starting in the middle and working outwards.

Quilting the Quilt

Quilting is the process of stitching the three layers together securely. As this is a beginner quilt, I have kept the quilting simple, using just stitch in the ditch and three other designs which you might like.

It is important to begin quilting in the middle of the quilt. This is also the most difficult part of the quilt to get to when you are using a domestic sewing machine. Position the quilt so that the central square is in the needle area. Make sure that the rest of the quilt is supported – either on the work surface or on your lap. Any quilt is heavy and you don't want to risk stretching the fabric by having the weight of it hanging towards the floor.

The part of the quilt to the right of the needle is usually the most problematic. There is a very limited area for a fairly large section of quilt. Some quilters roll that part of the quilt but I find that this restricts movement and I prefer to just bunch it up. The important section is the part immediately around the needle. That must be flat and the rest doesn't really matter.

I use a darning foot for my quilting but as this is all straight line quilting you could also use a walking foot. The darning foot shown here has a clear circle at the bottom so that you can see what you are doing at all times. I think you can just see that there is a spring going up the length of the foot – this allows the foot to move up and down over the fabric, so allowing it to move more freely.

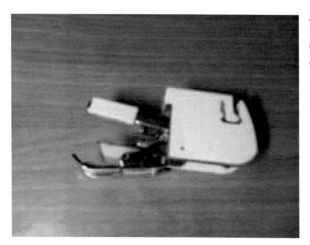

This is a walking foot which is intended for quilting straight lines, again allowing the fabric to move more freely because that lever at the top is positioned to raise the foot each time the needle rises.

The first (and probably most important) quilting that I have used on this quilt is stitch in the ditch quilting around every quilt block. This is straight line stitching along the seam lines, working with the patchwork quilt layer on top. You don't actually need to quilt around each block individually – quilting a grid of lines across the width and length of the quilt will end up enclosing each quilt block.

Begin in the middle of the quilt on one edge of the central quilt block and sew a line of stitching down to the bottom of the quilt, following the seam lines. Repeat with a line of stitching down the side of the next block and continue until all the blocks in the lower half of the quilt have vertical lines on each side. Turn the quilt around and quilt vertical lines beside all the blocks in the top half of the quilt.

Return to the middle of the quilt and sew lines of stitching between the blocks in the horizontal direction. When you have finished you should have a complete grid of quilting lines covering the entire quilt, with each quilt block enclosed by lines of quilting.

What you have just done is stabilise each area of the quilt. This is the absolute minimum of quilting that you should do. How close together you need to have lines of quilting depends on two things – the wadding that you have used and the look that you want for your quilt. If the quilting lines are too far apart you run the risk of the wadding sagging within the quilt sandwich. Most waddings specify the most distance that you should allow – usually somewhere between 4" and 8" but you should check for the particular wadding that you are using. The other factor is the personal preference one – do you want lots of very close quilting or not?

If you don't want too much quilting, you could just add further lines of quilting halfway across each quilt block. This would give you a grid of about 5" squares.

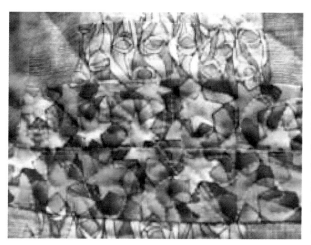

My choice was to use meander quilting on all the blue sections of the quilt. This doesn't show up very well in the photos, but it is the simplest form of free motion quilting – just a series of curves and loops made small or large depending on how dense you want the quilting to be. What I was aiming for was to pull together all the blue sections so that they would be seen as blocks of colour rather than segments of colour within each quilt block.

Having highlighted the blue sections, I then wanted diagonal lines to follow the general lines of the blue shapes. The simplest way to do this was by quilting another grid, but this one set on the diagonal. Mark all the lines in one direction first and sew them. Then mark the lines in the other diagonal and sew them. I find that this system is easier to work with – when I have marked the lines in both directions I can get confused as to which general direction I'm following when the entire quilt is scrunched up around my sewing machine. This can lead to marked lines being missed and it's always a nuisance to have to go back just to do the odd lines or parts of lines that you have missed.

In order to draw the lines, I used the cream squares in the middle of each quilt block as a guide. By placing my ruler so that the edge went across the diagonals of these squares I could draw lines following the diagonal.

These lines were about 7" apart, so I then drew another set of lines between them, setting my ruler at 3.1/2" from the lines that I had already drawn.

With all of this quilting, both the grid lines and the meander quilting, I left the quilt border free. Here I wanted a design with curves as there are so many straight lines throughout the quilt. I chose a simple flower with a circle cut out in the middle and cut it out in card so that I could use it as a template to mark the fabric.

To give some more interest to the design, I centred the flower first on the yellow border and then on the medium blue border so that the flowers moved up and down along the length of the border.

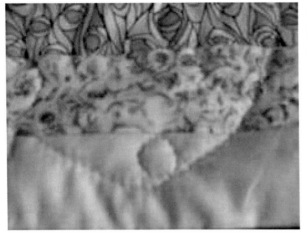

I drew all the flower shapes on to the quilt border using a fabric marker. After I had quilted each flower I moved on to the next flower using a curved line with a little loop in it. In that way I could keep the quilting continuous.

You will notice that the binding is already on in these photos of the quilt border. This should be the last step after all the quilting is complete, but in fact I find it difficult to quilt right into the edge of the quilt even though it has been basted. Sometimes it's easier to bind the quilt first and then finish the quilting on the border.

Quilt Binding

Cutting requirements

Eight 2.1/2" strips of fabric cut across the width of fabric.

Binding the quilt

The next step is one that I always do because I find that it gives me a neater edge to the quilt: hand baste around the edge of the quilt. I find that hand basting allows me to smooth both the top and backing fabric flat as I sew. Once this is done you can trim the excess backing and wadding so that all three layers line up.

Join binding strips by placing two strips at right angles to each other with right sides together. Sew along the diagonal of the square where the two strips overlap. Trim the excess triangles of fabric ¼" from the seam. These photos show a binding made using two different fabrics because it is more easy for you to see what I have done. The photos using black fabric only are not nearly as clear as these.

The binding strip then opens up into a straight line, but the diagonal seam makes the binding less bulky when it is sewn to the quilt edge. Pressing this seam open will also help to reduce bulk.

Press the binding strip in half along its length so that you end up with a double strip 1.1/4" wide.

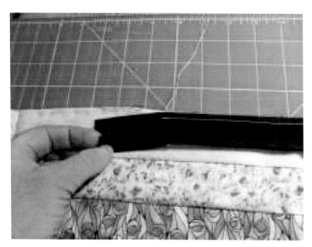

Place one end of the binding on the quilt top about half way down one of the edges. The fold of the binding should be towards the middle of the quilt and the raw edges in line with the raw edges of the quilt. Leave a trailing edge of an inch or two and begin sewing the binding to the quilt edge using a ¼" seam.

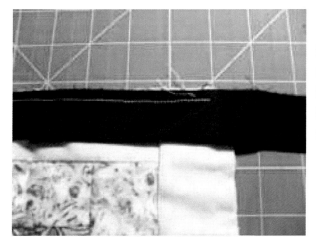

Stop sewing ¼" from the quilt corner and remove the quilt from the sewing machine. Lay down on the work surface with the binding stretching out in a straight line to the right of the quilt.

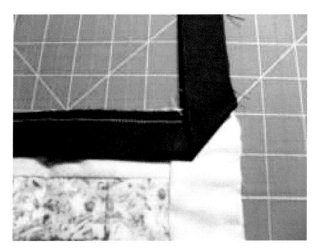

Fold the binding up away from the quilt so that it forms a diagonal fold on the corner of the quilt and the binding is now following the line of the next edge of the quilt to be bound.

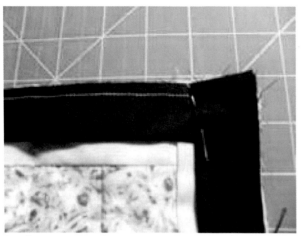

Holding the binding at the corner in place with your finger, fold it back down to continue along the second edge of the quilt. This second fold in the binding should be in line with the top of the quilt. Pin in place and then put the quilt back in the sewing machine and continue sewing from the corner along the length of the second edge of the quilt. Repeat the folding at each corner and continue till you are back to the first edge where you began to add the binding.

Stop sewing a few inches from the first edge of the binding. Trim the binding so that the two ends overlap by about an inch.

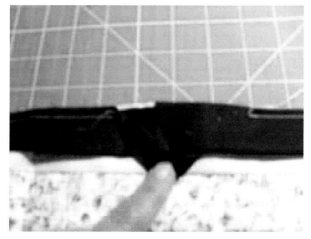

Turn under a small hem on one end of binding – I find it easiest to do this on the left hand (blue) binding strip.

Lay the lower layer of the left hand binding on the quilt edge but hold the top layer open. Place the end of the right hand binding across the left hand binding so that it will fit inside the fold.

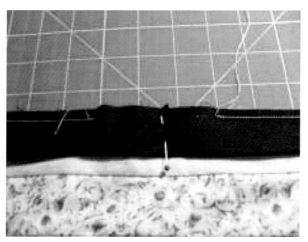

Lower the top layer of the left hand binding down so that it covers the right hand binding. As you can see, you have tidied away all the raw edges now. Sew across the gap in the stitching along the edge of the quilt so that the binding is attached to the entire edge of the quilt.

Flip the binding to the back of the quilt and slipstitch it to the back of the quilt.

At the corners, smooth the binding gently away from the quilt and then flip the binding down for the next edge and continue slipstitching. This will give you a neat mitred corner.

Continue sewing the binding to the back of the quilt until you get back to the beginning. Slipstitch the seam where the two pieces of binding were tucked together at the end of the binding.

That completes the log cabin quilt. At this stage I normally put the quilt straight in the washing machine as all the fabric has had such a lot of handling while you have been making it.

You can find more patterns and tutorials at my website: www.ludlowquiltandsew.co.uk.

Made in United States
North Haven, CT
15 February 2022

16140433R00022